This book belongs to:
www.cowboydogseries.com

Text by Mary Stern
Illustrations and book design by Anna-Maria Crum

CURRENT PRINTING
10 9 8 7 6 5 4 3 2 1

Library of Congress Cataloging – in Publication Data
Stern, Mary
    Country Critters by Mary Stern; illustrations by Anna-Maria Crum. 32 p. cm.
Summary: Ethan, Grandma, and Cowboy Dog go for a walk in the country where they see many animals.
ISBN: 978-0-9801602-1-5
1. Nature – Juvenile Literature. I. Stern, Mary. II. Title.

The illustrations for this book were done in acrylics on illustration board.

Printed and bound in USA.

For information, contact Mary Stern at www.cowboydogseries.com.

Part of the proceeds of this book will be donated to a charity that promotes reading to children as a part of early childhood development.

To my mother who read to me and gave me a love of reading and books.

Eileen Ramsey
1915 - 2009

www.cowboydogseries.com

Grandma!
Let's take cowboy dog for a run.
Being outdoors with you is fun.

You get her hat and I'll get my cape;
together we'll head out and make
our escape.

Let's walk down the road
and see what we spy.
We'll find birds and animals
if we try.

I spy a snake slithering into the reeds.
Hiding itself beneath the weeds.

Look up in the tree
at the great horned owl.
He's scouting around
and preparing to prowl.

Let's sit by the creek and take a rest;
and watch the birds building their nest.

The bluebirds add twig after twig,
making their nest nice and big.

I spot a hawk soaring high in the air.
He is riding the winds without a care.

I see a toad jump
and I shout EEK!
It hops away
to swim in the creek.

We splash in the water
and up jumps a trout.
It swims to the surface
and wiggles about.

Cowboy dog nudges us to move on.
If we wait much longer the sun will be gone.

Along the trail we spy a mouse.
She sees us coming and runs to her house.

Crossing the road is a fox with her kit.
She moves along so they won't get hit.

We're almost back home
so let's sit on the log
and discuss our adventures
with cowboy dog.

The toad, the mouse, and the snake startled me;
but not the birds that were in the tree.

I liked the fish swimming by my toe.
It came to the surface then dived down below.

I know the owl and hawk are birds of prey,
but I like watching them anyway.

Cowboy dog was a good guide.
She ignored the fox and stayed by our side.

The animals were fun and the birds were too,
but mostly I like spending time with you.

Me too, Ethan.